the I LOVE

LUCY

Guide to Life

the I LOVE **LUCY**
Guide to Life

WISDOM FROM LUCY AND THE GANG!

by Elisabeth Edwards

with Lucie Arnaz

RUNNING PRESS
PHILADELPHIA • LONDON

9   8   7   6   5   4   3   2   1
Digit on the right indicates the number of this printing

Library of Congress Control Number: 2004118275

ISBN 0-7624-2402-8

Edited by Greg Jones
Typography: AdLib BT, Clarendon, ChurchwardBruD, Murray Hill, Parade, Univers, and Zapf Dingbats

This book may be ordered by mail from the publisher.
Please include $2.50 for postage and handling.
But try your bookstore first!

Running Press Book Publishers
125 South Twenty-second Street
Philadelphia, Pennsylvania 19103-4399

Visit us on the web!
www.runningpress.com

Introduction

♥

On October 15, 1951, Lucille Ball, Desi Arnaz, Vivian Vance, and William Frawley made television history as they stepped on stage before a live audience for the premiere episode of the *I Love Lucy* show. Since that date, this classic show has never been off the air and is still seen today, 47 years later, in dozens of countries around the world. It is, in fact, the most re-run television show in history.

The secret behind the longevity of the show is its humanity. The Ricardos and the Mertzes taught the world about love, friendship, and loyalty. Whether at Kramer's Kandy Kitchen wrapping chocolates, in Los Angeles rubbing elbows with the stars, or in Italy stomping grapes, this fabulous foursome always managed to survive the wild antics that surrounded Lucy.

Desilu, too, LLC, and CBS Broadcasting Inc. are pleased to offer this book for the millions of fans, young and old, who have enjoyed this show for decades. Through the photos in this wonderful book, Lucy, Ricky, Ethel, and Fred spring to life to reveal their secrets of staying together through good times and bad.

Try to fit in with the crowd.

Imitation
is the sincerest form of
flattery.

Lucy's Fashion Tips

#1

DON'T LET THIS HAPPEN TO YOU!

GOOD **HYGIENE** AND A SENSE OF **STYLE** ARE **ESSENTIAL!**

Always

try to get 8 hours of

beauty sleep ...

. . . or face the
consequences!

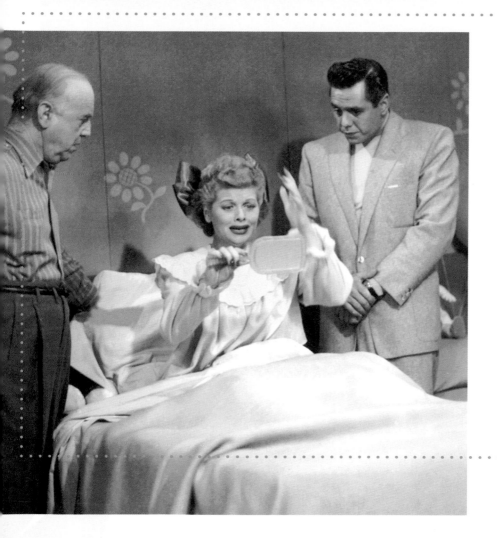

Get up on the
right side
of the bed.

Tell the truth (when it suits you!)

Lucy Ricardo:

the Queen of **SELECTIVE** honesty!

When caught, deny
everything!

If it tastes bad, it must be good for you!

When in doubt,
ask!

A trim tummy keeps hubby happy!

Never send a **woman** to do a man's job…

. . . she just might do it
better!

Lucy's Fashion Tips

#2

Accessorize!

quality time together...

If at first
you don't
succeed,
try, try
again.

Ricky, can I please be in your show? Please?
Please? Please? Pretty Please? Pretty please
with sugar on top? I swear I will never ask to
be in your show again. Oh please!!! You always
let the Mertz's in your show. Pleeeeeeeeeeease
RICKY! ARE YOU ... G TO ME? Waaaaaa
aaaaaaaaaaaaa ... aaaaaaaaaaaa!
Please please pp... se please. RICKY!
Please! Please! Pl... se! Please! Just
this one time, ... ve so much talen
and you just ... ease?Pretty
please with ... se? Please?
Pleeeeeeee ... eeeeeeease!
aaaaaaa ... aaaaa!

Where there's a will, there's a way!

Nobody likes a copycat.

MONKEY SEE, MONKEY DO!

If Lucy jumped off a bridge, would you?

If your name happens to be

Ethel Mertz,

the answer is probably YES!

If you want something

done wrong,

do it yourself!

Home repair jobs are for
the birds!

#3

Dress
for
Success!

Never be a
phone gossip!

Crank calls are
never amusing.

Misery **loves**
company.

Laugh, and the world laughs with you...

. . .Weep, and you
weep alone.

But, sometimes, a good cry **does** make it all better.

A smile is just a frown turned upside-down!

Mean what you say!

Ricky Ricardo

When he says "No," he means "NO!!!"

#4

DON'T BE A FASHION VICTIM!

Crime
doesn't pay.

SEE
NO EVIL

HEAR
NO EVIL

SPEAK
NO EVIL

Lucy's Fashion Tips

#5

A nice tan
will add that
healthy
glow!

Get in touch with your
inner child.

You're **only** as old as you **look**.

A penny saved is a penny earned.

Fred Mertz:

self-proclaimed cheapskate!

Always leave
instructions
when putting someone
else in charge.

Beauty

is in the eye of the beholder!

Lucy's Fashion Tips

#6

Clothes

MAKE

the man!

Lucy's Fashion Tips

#7

Well, clothes don't

ALWAYS

make the man.

Beware

of princes—they can be

charming!

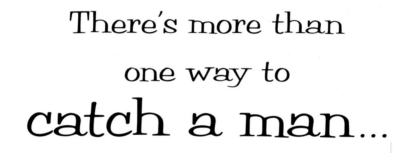

There's more than

one way to

catch a man...

. . . but only **one** way to **keep** him!

Don't forget to remove
the lens cap!

Patience is a virtue.

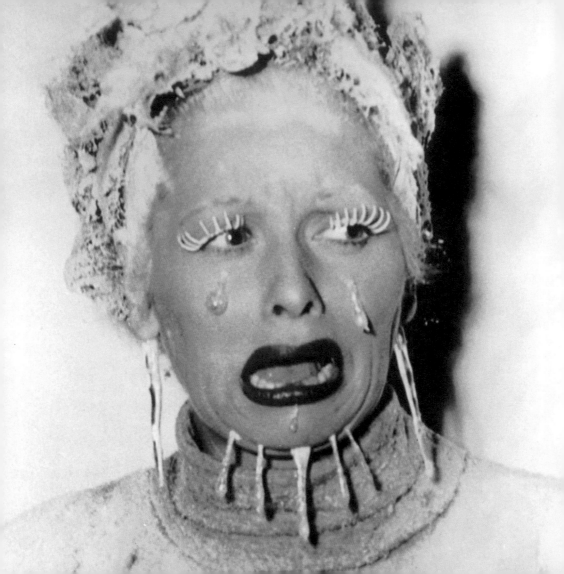

Always keep your cool.

WATCH YOUR TEMPER!

Channel
your anger.

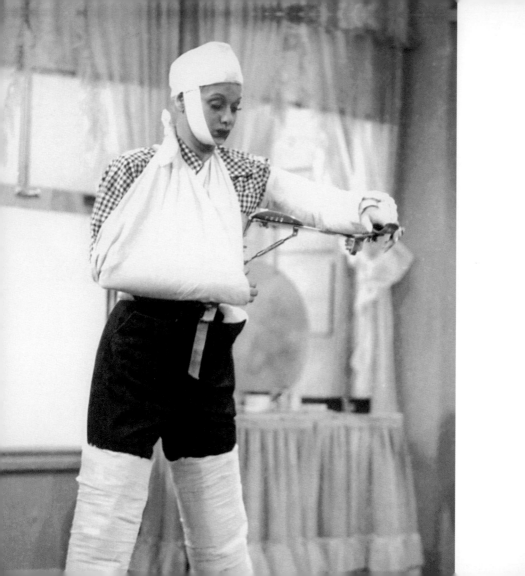

Prey on the

sympathy

of others.

Ladies,

wax that

facial hair

before it's too late!

Don't

chickens

they

ha

count
your

before

tch!

Follow these tips and
you will live

happily ever
after!